ANCHOR
BOOKS

CELEBRATIONS IN VERSE
FROM THE SOUTH EAST

Edited by

Sarah Andrew

First published in Great Britain in 2001 by
ANCHOR BOOKS
Remus House,
Coltsfoot Drive,
Peterborough, PE2 9JX
Telephone (01733) 898102

HB ISBN 1 85930 961 5
SB ISBN 1 85930 966 6

FOREWORD

For many of us the medium of poetry offers us a voice - a voice to speak out and let others know what we feel, think and desire. It is the vital bridge of communication that lets us share our innermost thoughts and messages on life to people who may need that vital surge of poetic inspiration.

Each of the chosen poems have been specifically favoured from a large selection of entries sent. As always, editing proved to be a difficult task and as the editor, the final selection was mine.

Celebrations In Verse From The South East is a unique collection of poetry and verse written in a variety of styles and themes, brought to us from many of today's modern and traditional writers, who reside in this area. The poems are easy to relate to and encouraging to read, offering engaging entertainment to their reader.

This delightful collection is sure to win your heart, making it a companion for life and perhaps even earning that favourite little spot upon your bookshelf.

Sarah Andrew
Editor

CONTENTS

THE CLOSURE OF PRIORY ROAD COMMUNITY EDUCATION CENTRE

Priory Road was once a school,
 It was a splendid place.
Hastings Sec Mod Boys it was,
 The name had no disgrace.

The Grammar School and Priory Road,
 Decided to combine.
At the William Parker Comp,
 A marriage almost divine.

That left the old school buildings,
 Standing ready to decay.
Till Hastings College came along,
 To use them day by day.

Community Education,
 That was the latest craze.
Adults learning in their neighbourhood,
 Their talents would amaze.

French and Spanish, English Lit,
 And writing most creative.
Dressmaking and floral art,
 Or speaking German like a native.

The buildings have that homely feel,
 Us students really like.
And everyone's so friendly,
 Staff and students both alike.

And now this place will close its doors,
 The courses relocated.
We'll be so sad: The fun we've had;
 Here, being educated.

Cliff De Meza

DECEMBER ROSE

Alone she stands in upright pose
Defying winter's icy blast
A single budded rose
Her dainty bloom to Heavenward's cast.

The frost may chill, the wind may moan
The earth held fast in winter's grip
But still she bravely stands alone
And dares the frost her petals nip.

I gaze upon her beauty there
And think upon the summer gone.
Should I pick her, leave the rose bush bare?
'twould be a pity leave her struggling on.

And so amidst the mass of thorns
That threaten to entwine my hands
Carefully from that bush is torn
That single rose, at my command.

Into a vase she now is placed
That bright red rose, so strong, erect
My Christmas table now shall grace,
From all adornments, stands select.

Her beauty soon will fade, I know
Her perfume no more tantalise my nose,
But when the summer comes again
I'll remember then, *December rose!*

Elizabeth Hale

DANCE WITH A GREEN BALLOON

The seaside carnival, with swirling fun,
Its floats and clowns, its riotous disguise,
Excited voices, beauty queens and bands,
Was over now; the vivid day was done.

With long, low waves the quiet evening tide
Crept imperceptibly towards the shore;
The cooling sand was lost in its embrace
While, high above, a lonely seagull cried.

Lank, dry seaweed, round every rocky pool,
Took life in flowing tresses, glossy, dark.
The hot, dry, sandy smell became a tang
Of boats and salty nets, sea-washed and cool.

Faint music came from somewhere out of sight,
With lingering echoes of the lively day,
While, idly floating past the band-stand, came
A green balloon, abandoned to the night.

Lifting it, with unselfconscious grace,
A little girl, who wore a yellow dress,
Danced with it upon the platform there;
She danced alone, absorbed, with grave young face.

With slender arms outstretched to reach her toy
Her gentle fingers round the smooth, green curves,
She somehow captured all the deep regrets
We feel, when losing some departing joy.

The music stopped; she softly walked away
And vanished in the ever growing shade,
The green balloon forgotten once again,
As sunset stole the dying summer day.

Margaret Ballard

THE PRIESTESS OF LONGING

The spiritual needs of people
Are not catered for under a steeple
The Priestess of power comes from nature
To help true feelings and nurture

A belief in the holistic powers of the Earth
To shine through with bright wealth
In a tradition of positive learning
To help the lonely and yearning

And free up shrouded emotions
Kept chained up for so long
Who's to say what's really wrong
And what's so right for a thousand commotions
The Priestess means love and comes near

To whisper in your ear about the profound
As a spirit enters your soul without a sound
To help save the future of nature
Within the ancient heart of rapture

The flowing hair and cloak of white
Soon appears to tell you of the night
A dream or illusion it may seem
Only time and truth will set the scene.

Tim Sharman

OH WOE TO BE UNFIT!

I walked a mile then found a seat,
Time to rest my weary feet.
Only a mile, is that all I've done?
It really feels like twenty-one!
I'm twenty-five stone and not a pound less,
I've more blubber than a whale I must confess!
So it's off to the gym to shed a bit,
Put on my trainers and grab my kit!
Soon I'll be the handsome devil I was before,
And instead of a mile I'll walk ten more!

Caroline Dean

PLAYTIME

We're a couple of widows, we live quite alone
two of the most erratic people, you've ever known.

Whenever we meet, it's always the same
we discard what we're doing, we must have a game.

No need to ask, cribbage, or what will it be
it's backgammon for Phyll, and backgammon for me.

Phyll needs to face Mecca, then she's sure she can win
it's one of those things, at which I just grin.

While we are playing, the world's put to rights
leaving out politics, it has lead to fights.

We debate Telecom, British Gas and our shares
the game's to relax us, to dispel all our cares.

Wake up Phyll, it's five - three to you
though usually it's a double six, double four or a two.

I'd love to throw doubles, as often as Phyll
the dice just will not, bend to my will.

Doubles roll out, one after the other
there are times - when Phyll I could smother.

We're not too polite, when the game we are losing
and not too particular with words we are using.

We don't play for money, use a kitty or pot
Phyll's a good loser - believe me I'm not.

We'll play on for ages, sometimes, to level the score
with a little more concentration, not like before.

At the end of the game, we check up to see
who's won this session, is it Phyll, no it's me.

We love our backgammon - it's a great deal of fun
who cares, at the end of the day, who had won.

Zena

THE SEAGULL

When wild winds render the clouds asunder
Scaling the sky with swoops and swings
Wending the world's wide ways I wander
With sunlit wonder upon my wings

Nowhere welcome in winter weather
Never the warmth of the woods for me
Nothing kindly to beak and feather
Only the clean cold cliffs and the sea.

John D H Soper

ETERNAL

Here comes another one, just as before
Hissing and crashing on the same soaked shore,
Roll after roll, drop after drop
Blue at the centre, white at the top
Identical each in the way they behave
Wave, after wave, after wave, after wave.

Sunlight sparkles at the top of each crest,
In motion the ocean never at rest
Since time began - today - evermore
The relentless wash of the sea on the shore,
The rhythm and power, the salt in the spray
Under moon, under sun, every night, every day.

Jill Gunter

THE WOUND

Feelings rushing,
Blood pumping,
Head aching,
Chest tight.

The pain comes as one,
One sharp stab to the heart,
Once removed it leaves you,
Empty and alone.

The pain never ending,
Always there to haunt you,
With any glimmer of hurt,
The pain comes flowing back,
Stabbing harder than ever before.

When the would heals,
You endlessly wonder,
If or when it will be,
Ripped open once again.

To feel the pain running,
Into your heart, body and soul,
Leaving you weak and defenceless.

Nathalie Coleman

ODE TO ANNA

A fabulous feeling of freedom,
freedom of the mind.
Like I've left the cage I've lived in,
a hundred miles behind.
To procreate would be too base,
for my new friend, moonface,
but her company is divine,
it leaves me feeling fine.
Though our friendship may fade,
it will not be forgotten,
because in my mind,
I will always find,
the lady with a hamster,
tattooed on her behind.

Danny Coleman

CHILD'S PLAY

Their nerves on edge, the war was far from won,
another push, the messy business, over and done.
The generals used that phrase, to urge them on,
they know now, it was just a verbose, clever con.
'Come on lads, up and at 'em', went the shout,
on the attack, from trenches they piled out.
Facing an unseen enemy, with trepidation,
fighting, for the glory of the British nation.
Some lived, many died, but most of all,
so I'm told, almost everybody cried.

In the long grass, my enemy waited, ready.
Then my grandad shouted at me,
'Come on Johny and don't forget teddy.'

Andy Monnacle

DON'T GIVE UP

I know that at the moment
It doesn't seem worthwhile
To carry on with mundane chores
Or even just to smile

But just around the corner
Although it's out of sight
Is a brighter spell just waiting
To grab you very tight.

I sometimes think life tests us
It pushes us all to
A limit that just leaves us
Feeling lousy, feeling blue.

You are strong enough to raise your head
But time is all you need
You have to sometimes ride a storm
You cannot act with speed.

So don't give up, you'll see in time
These days they will be passed
Look forward, take each day that comes
This sadness will not last.

Angela Fuller

THEIR EXPLANATION

Well I can't really say, sometimes she's OK.
She will laugh and be happy.
But then she shouts and just gets ratty.
And yes, without a doubt
I just can't do anything right . . .
Whatever I say or do it always ends up in a fight.

Oh maybe tomorrow you never know
This depression may just go
She'll wake up one morning
Tomorrow I hope
And all these things hanging over her
Will go up in smoke!

I hear you talking to our friends
They say, 'But won't this ever end?'
It will, you say, but I don't know when.

You look so caring when you explain
It's no child's plaything.
'Depression's no game, she's ill,'
You find it hard to say.
You pray for me everyday.

I also find it hard to explain
I feel like dying because I can't stand the pain . . .
The pain that keeps me from my sleep,
The pain that makes me weep . . .

'I let her know I love her and I need her so
But she's so unhappy, she just tells me to go.
It's been going on now for a very long time,
This terrible illness in her mind.

I'll cheer her up, I'll tell her you called
I'll give her your love and best wishes too,
Oh I forget don't tell her *I told you!*'

Jayne Harsum

THE STORMY DAY

Clouds bumping, like bumper cars in the sky
Wind whistles, like a kettle,
Puddles like paddling pools on the path
It's a stormy, stormy day.

The trees bow down to the breeze
The wind snatches your hat and carries it away,
Hailstones fall, like acorns falling off an oak tree.
Then the rain came out to play.
It's a stormy, stormy day.

People run into their houses for shelter,
Umbrellas get put inside out by the gale,
Tornadoes twist and twirl like a spinning top,
It's a stormy, stormy day.

Steven Moulding

Beyond Tears And Care
Aberystwyth In December

('Hic quos durus arnor crudeli tabe peredit
Secreti celant calles et myrtea circum
Silva tegit; curae non ipsa in morte relinquunt.' Vergil)

What a sight for weary eyes is accord!
Herein is life, herein is more than flesh and bones,
While the whole creation in labour groans
For the coming of the Lord.

On a day like this, so mild, so fair,
How might it be I sojourned there?
The sea leisurely washing pebbled strands -
Timeless, unhindered, it washes still -
But then bewintered, bereft of birds,
Mustering, ushering souls in droves,
Sorrowful, sent from sundry lands.
I often mused, reclining in my chair,
Whether the lashes stretched this far -
And I was struck in soothe, in awe,
For I hardly knew such grief before,
Which comes in Stygian waves.

Blue, eternal blue, the sky's expanse
Where Lethe flows, and shades run back,
Who, merciless, threw down their tears
And watered heaven with their fears -
Embellished embers of parting day,
The swan-span clouds have more sense.

Gentle waves upon a distant shore
Fall, awaiting the silent Behest;
All is still, yet all is night -
Let the past relent and sigh no more.

J D T Chipperfield

A CHILD OF WAR

I glimpsed up and saw your face
Such beauty is so sad a place
Your smile gave the courage to me
To swallow my fear and do my duty.

A soldier's life is so throught
With horrors that we were not taught
How could they
Indiscriminently spray
The evil from their guns
Into all, even as they run.

How sick I feel from deep within
How horrified by man's great sin
Yet you, a child can smile.
Innocence and faith, I've none
My courage was the gun.
Your simplicity has reached my heart
Where healing has to start.

I glimpsed again afraid to see
Oh, such sadness look at me
My eyes sting, the tears flow free

If those that say, life is but dust
That they alone are great, they have no fear
Could understand that humans rust
And even they may shed a tear,
When their time is up will they then fear?
I glimpsed up and saw your face,
Such beauty in so sad a place.

A M Seago

JUST FOR A WHILE

I sit by the window
And watch you fly by
You sit in the treetops
And dance in the sky
You fly with such grace
And it makes me smile
For I once was like you
But just for a while

I danced in the moonlight
And under the stars
I flew through the wind
To my lover's arms
And all of my memories
They make me smile
For I once was like you
But just for a while.

For now I am older
My legs do not run
My wings do not flutter
My flying is done
But watching the birds
They make me smile
For once I was like them
But just for a while

Paula Whatley

A SUMMER'S TALE

The sun that slants soft light in little rays,
Its dappled beams fond images displays.
The sticklebacks that dart on home-spun wings,
In flight away from many grosser things,
And then dart back again, as if in scorn,
From out of shadows into waters' warm.

The flycatcher, which nests in abbey wall,
With undulating flights, that rise and fall,
As high on summer air it sets its seal,
And on the wing it plucks another meal.

The honey bee with sweetness in its flight,
Which hinges on the flowers in great delight,
It knows that it's with nature not at odds,
And from the tendril, sucks the food of gods.

To hear the lark trill soft on summer breeze,
Listening to the wind consort the trees.
Ah! Meadow lark, what sweeter voice can sing
And to a harassed heart such warmth can bring.

Old owl, that's cloistered way up there,
Gives not a hoot, suffice it sits to stare,
And blink a canny eye, just now and then,
In uncommitted thoughts of beasts and men.

Alistair A Murch

THE FARM CAT

Mary went into the barn
And cried - 'Oh is that a rat?'
When something furry flowed over her feet.
No, it's only the frantic farmyard cat.

Mary looked round the barn
And heard a hiss and a spat.
T'was the feathery barn owl she'd disturbed
In her search for the fearsome farmyard cat.

Mary climbed straw in the barn
For she'd heard a pittery pat.
A tabby cat nestles with kittens five.
Issue of the friendly farmyard cat.

Mary brought into the barn
Some milk and a bowl of sprat.
For she wanted to find the handsome tom.
And stroke the formidable farmyard cat.

Mary saw him in the barn,
He appeared so sleek and fat
As he slowly approached her outstretched palm.
She caressed the fearless farmyard cat.

Mary stayed in the barn
On a bale of straw she sat.
Slumbering on her lap in comfort lay
The frantic, fearsome, friendly, formidable, fearless
    farmyard cat.

Judith Simmons

SPIDER

Spider, spider - in the half-light,
hairy body and puncture bite;
stillness's master gives no hint
of most unnerving forms of sprint.

So many eyes no limpid pools,
no cutlery - just mandibles;
eight legs secure profound embrace -
all prey becomes an empty case.

Often seen - but more often hid -
scientists have named it arachnid;
with no view from an 'insider'
reason none to kill a spider.

Legend says, if it so should die,
the killer returns as a fly,
whose nervous reincarnation
ends in fluid deprivation!

A W Wells

HECHTSEE KUESTEIN

Snow on barren wilder kaiser
Fir covered slopes below,
Give way to lush green meadows
Where alpine flowers grow.
Purple orchids, at home quite rare
Seems to flourish everywhere!
Immaculate chalets, some new, some old
Each bedecked with flowers bold,
Each village with its own church spire
A haven once, when times were dire,
Still a refuge, come what may,
A sacred spot, to kneel and pray.
Smiling faces, air like wine,
Sparkling rivers, spruce and pine,
Everything, so fresh and clean,
Clothed in nature's special green,
Happy memories to take away,
Hoping we'll return some day.

Dorothy Puttick

SEVEN DAYS

Ever wondered, when, where, why
There is the land, the sea, the sky
The sun, the moon and us too
The animals, not from the zoo.

Before all this, once said a man
'I'll create a new world, if I can'
And with a wave of staff and rod
Began creation, his name was God.

'Now firstly I'll create the light
The light is day, the darkness night
So proud am I that I can say
'I've just invented the first day'.

The second day he made the air
Clear, like there was nothing there
And with a sparkle in his eye
Professed 'This air I'll call the sky'.

Next came the water, so pleased was he
Painted it blue and called it sea
Such strong hands with all his worth
Gathered soil and called it earth.

Cried out loud 'This is such fun
Let's have the stars, the moon, the sun'
Closed his eyes and made a wish
'Now let the sea be full with fish'.

'What's left to do, what's missing still
A voice to carry on my will'
He bowed his head and said with grace
'Behold here is the human race'.

The seventh day he made and blessed
A holy day for prayer and rest
To carry on the work he'd done
Sent down from heaven, his only son.

In seven days God made the world
Now all his aspirations unfurled
So if you wonder when, where, why
God made it all for you and I.

Steve Morrison

ODE TO A VODKA AND LIME

I sit in the dusk of my life
with a drink in my hand,
wondering where life has gone
that I'd dreamed and planned.
Is it that I think, a drink
will cover the scars,
will bring new hope
give me fresh thoughts to my stale breath?
The smile I show my friends
the life so full,
do I convince myself, perhaps,
with a drink.
The laughter that emptily echoes
in my head,
the spinning room as I lay in my bed,
I wonder if this is what it's all about
the haze of uncertainty
the whoosh of insecurity
like ping-pong in my brain.
Oh for peace,
oh for tranquillity,
oh for a drink.

Madeline Gibbins

FEELINGS OF LIFE

Darkness is a wonder a mystery untold
A soft and subtle pleasure never bright or bold
A careless tender whisper of secrets new and old
Spirits cold and evil like the soul you once sold.

Sunlight is a gift from the stars above
A glimmer of happiness a telltale sign of love
A sweet and scared messenger high up like a dove
A mystery of power that holds you like a glove.

Love is a passion that comes from the soul
A everlasting feeling a complete one time goal
A touch of tenderness that warms you like hot coal
A soft warm feeling like hugging a doll.

Hate is a terror that smothers the heart
A feeling of loneliness that burns from the start
A cold sensation that hits like a dart
A silent corrupter in great works of art.

Emma Russell

WILD POTIONS

Wild potions made up behind factory gates
styled potions fused to spoil our view
mild potions odourless set fire to my throat
wild potions boxed then shipped by boat.

Wild potions patented
I'll save a flower.
Wild potions lament
another acid shower.

Wild potions made up behind factory gates,
you asked
I answered to this I hate.
Wild potions made up behind factory gates
destructive hackers.
Dot. com.
Relate?

Wild potions abased
styled potions excused
wild potions diluted.
Wild potions refused,
I'll save a flower.

Wild potions patented
I'll save a flower.
Wild potions lament
another acid shower.

L D Ashman

MY GARDEN

My garden is my favourite place.
The place where I can turn my face.
Away from the fast insidious pace,
That now besets the human race.

My garden is my pleasant spot.
The spot I like when it's warm and hot.
Where I can go and read a lot,
And for worldly worries care not one jot.

My garden is my pride and joy,
My thoughts and emotions I can employ.
Planting, weeding, cutting grass.
Slowly or quickly, time will pass.

My garden is my quiet release.
Tranquillity, beauty, and profound peace.
What pleasure to find green shoots peeping through.
To hoe, and dig out a weed or two.

My garden is my happiest haven.
Where I can plan my life without complication.
I can dream grand dreams, that won't come true.
But never-the-less I can think they do.

My garden is my favourite place.
The place where I can turn my face.
Against the fast insidious pace,
That now besets the human race.

Jenny Elsen

AUTUMN

How the wind howls round the chimney tonight,
Autumn is here, winter is in sight,
Patter, pitter-patter on the windowpane,
Oh goodness, surely not more rain.

Sighing I think of the summer just past,
What a pity it doesn't last,
Didn't start until June this year
Nine months before it comes back I fear.

Lovely summer evenings seem now like a dream,
Sitting in the garden eating strawberries and cream,
Watching the swallows darting over head,
Ducks squabbling over the bread.

Feeling the sea rippling over my toes,
The tide's going out, I wonder where it goes?
Basking in the sun, trying to get a tan,
It's getting so hot, I wish I'd brought a fan.

But now it is autumn and I must do my best,
To grin and bear it like the rest,
We can take it, we Brits are tough,
We know how to take the smooth with the rough!

Pat Sandaver

GROWING OLD

They say that life begins at forty
But that's not completely true.
More likely 'enjoy yourself while you are young'.
Schooldays are not necessarily the best either,
If you are lucky only in hindsight.
Forty really is a good age
But if you begin your life here,
Then, well, you have left it too late.

At fifty a computer is triggered somewhere
And Saga arrives uninvited on the doormat.
Never, never, never.
Age.
Growing old.
Being old.
Has nothing to recommend it.
I watched my parents grow old
Silently monitoring their developing frailties.
Saw them suffer in developing pains.
'Wear and tear' the doctor said.
There are no cures for the elderly.

Timothy Blewitt

JOY OF THE ORGAN

There was a lady organist who never any moment missed
to play all day, for she would say, 'I love to learn another way.'
She practised there from ten to one because she said it was such fun.
Then down to the local pub where they have such lovely grub,
washed down with a pint of bitter, 'Good' she said 'I'm feeling fitter.'
Then rolling back to her console where she played to please them all.
Classic, jazz and even pop, the vicar soon began to hop.
The choir and all the congregation left from their appointed station
and joined the dance, they all did prance, all except for Missis Lance.
It seemed that she was rather quaint, for she fell down in a faint.
They revived her with some gin, 'Oh dear,' she said 'this is a sin,
I've been teetotal all my life and now will be in for strife
when I reach the pearly gates where Peter deals out all the fates.
Just for one quite little sin, will he be kind and let me in?'
'Now what a lovely drink I had, to waste surely would be bad.
May I have another sip?' She drank it up and was so quick down
the aisle she had a skip, that somebody who saw her said, 'Look just
there, but have a care we can glimpse her underwater!'
And from that day this church of fame was dedicated in the name
of He who lives in heaven on high, for the Bishop to decry
all gloomy hymns and psalms no more as often had been heard before.
And, people travelled from afar, some by train and some by car
to worship God and have some fun, with enjoyment everyone.

Joan Last

SEASONS

Soon the snow will melt away,
Passing by in its own way,
Raising forth - the flowers come,
In their beauty, silent, home,
Never changing, spring is given,
God's own gift of life . . .

South winds blow so warm and dry,
Underneath the clear blue sky,
Marvellous perfumes fill the air,
Mountains reaching high,
Eventide, so warm and still,
Roses out - upon a sill . . .

Avenues of rusty leaves,
Underneath the bearing trees,
Tens of thousands birds migrate,
Until they reach a warm climate,
Men prepare for long dark evenings,
Nurturing tales of summer . . .

Winds and snow and frosty mornings,
Icicles hang on barn and gate,
Never a wind has blown so cold,
Temperatures drop to minus eight,
Except for when we stop to stare,
Realising God's own beauty - there.

Hazel Langridge

MYSTERIOUS NIGHTS

The hub crashes through my mind, excited chatter
Nervous tongues - frightened minds.
Slowly as the dance unravels before us -
Peace brings the fearful eyes to order
Swaying this way and that,
Like a cobra she draws us into her trance.

Blank expressions, contorted minds try to reason
No use, we're lost to the sway of the talking head.
Under her chin I see the turkey's gobble,
Somewhere in the distance
Bob Dylan is singing an unrecognisable lyric.

Wondering just where the time went
Stunned, we pack our bags, reeling from the dance.
Blank faces confused minds,
See you next week a voice cried!
Silence! As they shuffle out and into the night.

Dinswill McDonald

THIS WONDROUS EARTH

They come from God, the wondrous things,
the trees, the flowers, the birds that sing.
And every little plant and weed,
the Lord doth grow them all from seed.
He sends the sun, the warmth, the rain,
to nurture every tiny grain.
He feeds the sheep to give us meat,
to make us strong each time we eat.

How is it that I fail to see,
the generous gifts from him to me.
The earth would just be barren land,
without the Lord to lend a hand.
Dear Jesus teach me not to long
for treasures which would do me wrong.
To look around, to be content,
with wonders that are heaven sent.

Margaret Stenson

A LIFE

Just after the war, my mum and dad
bought a guest house down by the sea,
I used to earn pocket money
by taking round the morning tea.
The spuds I'd peel for up to twenty-four
and the brass I'd clean on the big front door.
After laying the tables, if the weather was fine
down to beach I'd flee.

When I left school I went into an office
and sat at a desk all day,
It wasn't how I envisaged working
and twenty-five bob was meagre pay.
So I joined the army - Royal Engineers,
and enjoyed my time for five good years.
But when I'd served my time
and a demob suit they gave me,
I was eager to be off and away.

For a time I couldn't settle down
and life went in many directions,
Then I met a nurse on Brighton station one day,
to me she was perfection.
After eighteen months we decided to wed,
I got a good job to bring in the bread,
In time we had two smashing sons
who were brought up with love and affection.

They in turn married two lovely girls
and five grandchildren I must mention,
the next generation is well under way,
the natural family extension.

It gets no easier though to make a living,
I work just as hard - always striving.
But roll on the next twelve months I say,
then is the time I pick up my pension.

W R Barnham

A Song Of Life

The sky was filled with stars, and up above
    The moon, a silv'ry orb, shone brightly down;
A wind was softly sighing through the poplars
    And a sense of peace lay gently on the town.

I wandered slowly past the sleeping houses;
    My thoughts were ling'ring on the day just passed.
I stared up at the stars and bleakly wondered
    How they could shine when all my world had crashed.

The air was crisply cold and to my heart -
    A heart numbed by depression through the day -
It slowly brought a sense of hope, of courage,
    And pierced my brain to where frustration lay.

Had I shrunk from facing up to adverse setbacks?
    Had I thought my life so easily wooed and won?
Had the lesson to be learned against frustration
    Been given up before it had began?

The moonlight seemed to lighten on my failure -
    Seemed to show the world how puny mortals are.
I quickened up my pace, and hurried forward,
    To avoid the piercing twinkle of a star.

Ashamed, I then resolved to brace my shoulders,
    To face the future where so ere it lay.
I cast aside the sense of drab depression
    That had hung around my heart throughout the day.

I realised at last that through life's journey
    Though the world may scorn at times when things go wrong;
If your duty's nobly done and you have courage,
    Your life will prove to be a joyous song.

Joan Packwood

SPRING

Before the dawning of the day
Hark! What a welcome din!
Awaken there, the morn is fair
Spring has sprung again.

The 'dawn chorus' has awakened us
Our feathered friends can't wait
To collect feathers, wool and moss
And find a suitable mate.

The rootlets are spreading underground
The bulbs are shooting out.
Snowdrops, crocuses and daffodils
Have appeared above the ground.

Young calves are being born
And fed on their mother's milk
Young lambs will soon be frisking
All around the hills.

The rose trees and the garden shrubs
Are sprouting their blossoms and blooms.
They need a good, fertile soil
While still in earth's safe womb.

The gardener is preparing the ground
With fertiliser, manure and peat.
When the soil is ready
The sun provides the heat.

The sun is shining up above
The morning bright with cheer.
How wonderful to be alive
Now that spring is here.

Mary Buckley

SUSSEX BY THE SEA

I'd heard it in song,
Maybe sung along,
Oh to be there free,
Sussex by the Sea.

First as commuter,
Hearing train's hooter,
I came to the coast,
Heaven! Was my boast.

Local employment,
Extra time that meant,
The good Sussex air,
Could banish all care.

Early retirement,
My working life spent,
For my wife and me,
Sussex by the Sea.

D Spanton

LATE TREES

Almost a whole painter's palette
    is laid on these trees -
the city's eclipsed from this seat -
a ginkgo with a dancer's grace
    and loose yellow sleeves
of foliage curves to a praise
before a sumac's crimson flame
    against the dark hearth
of a garden fence, the huge plume
of a tulip tree and the rage
    of a sweet gum, stain
the dying light with their message:
a flame burns hotter on the wane.

It's an action painting in slow
    motion, the plant world
rehearsing for its goal below
and the leaves now leaving for home
    shame our rootless hues.
Dark trunks bear out the gliding gleam
holding against the clouds like birds
    for the frames are proud.
I would like to haunt with such words
as these poised trees can utter, huge
    on a city park,
the still heart of the centrifuge
where we who search recline and walk.

Chris White

THE REMOVAL VAN

The removal van
Came today,
All her bits and pieces,
Provisions
Good and bad
Bundled into the van,
The men laughing,
Handling things with a joke.

In my mind's eye,
I could see her still,
The little lady
In the garden
Tending the roses she loved,
Someone else
Will move in,
Her roses - in memory - will live on
And her loving hands
Still rest on them.

Madeline Chase

MY DREAM

I awoke one morning after a beautiful dream
And as I lay thinking about what I had seen,
I remembered a land of mountains and streams,
Such beauty can only be seen in dreams.
The mountains and fields were covered in snow
And as I stood and stared it made my heart glow.
The snow was so soft and so white,
It really was a most wonderful sight.
Sweet music seemed to come from the trees
As they swayed together in the gentle breeze,
I felt so free as I danced with bare feet,
I was so happy enjoying this wonderful treat.
My dress was flimsy, but I didn't feel cold,
All around me was beauty untold.
The sparkling sun made jewels in the snow
And the lovely bright colours were all aglow.
Suddenly, in the distance soft bells were ringing
Birds of every colour appeared and started singing.
Then, a little boy came from behind a tree
Saying, 'Come, come quickly with me
You have wandered much too far,
You must not see beyond your star,
I will show you the way back to Earth,
You are not yet ready for your second birth.'
Suddenly I awoke, as I had fallen back to sleep
And, of my life to come had been given a little peep.

Sylvia Gwilt

BLIZZARD

The snow comes swirling all around
It fills the air, it's on the ground
It's in my hair and in my face
I am confused, I lose my place.
It takes my breath, it takes my sight
I stumble left and stumble right.
Soon the flakes blot out the world
I twist and turn, but I am hurled
Into a silent, dark, white night
All alone with Nature's might.
I fight to keep my panic down
There is no sound but menace creeps
The white flood deepens and the world sleeps.
Then the silence is shattered,
Shrieks of a mindless wind fill the air
As the monster leaps fully out of its lair.
Of the world I know there is no trace
The flakes now madly fight and race
Around, around and up and down
The end of the world in its sinister sound.
I too shriek, lost in my fears.
Hands at my head to cover my ears.
My frenzied, desperate actions are futile
There is no escape and I fall,
Lost in the desolation of a white death.
Then I awake, and as I do, I shiver.

Pamela J Hinton

GRASS MONOLOGUE

I stand here, swaying in the wind,
In fear of being eaten by passing sheep.
All of my family and friends live in the same outside 'house'.

I watch the humans pick my fellow friends.
Every morning is a reflective mirror all around me,
Everyone all the same shade of green, identical to myself.

I cannot move myself to a better place,
My feet stuck in the wet soil,
Not being able to dodge human feet.

The torrential rain of the English countryside
Can beat and bully me,
But never knock me down.

The heat of the summer
I dread, although sunbathing turns me a lovely tanned brown.
I fear my future may be one of shrivelling and dying.

As an aeroplane screams overhead,
I smell the farmers spreading manure on their fields.

I am a blade of grass in a Sussex Downs' field,
Please do not trespass on my homeland.

Jason Button (13)

EVER CHANGING WORTHING

We've only lived in Worthing for about eight years,
Moving down from Horsham 'cause the prices there were fierce.
The house that we had chosen seemed to make us feel at ease,
It welcomed us and left enough to pay the legal fees.
There's everything around us from hospitals to schools,
The local shopping centre, cinema and pools.
Further inland are the downs with views of tranquil space,
An added bonus is the sea, an ever changing place.

Claire Shepherd

EXPECTANT

Deirdre said, 'Y-e-s,'
Then Deirdre said, 'No.'
Deirdre said, 'Bother!
    I really don't know.'

Deirdre stood up,
Then down Deirdre sat,
Deirdre reflected,
    'Can't keep doing that.'

Deirdre was nodding,
Then shaking her head;
Deirdre said, 'Dear me,
    I'm going to bed.'

Deirdre lay down,
Then sat up erect;
Deirdre remarked
    That it had no effect.

Deirdre is breathing -
Gasps come and go;
Deirdre is trying
    To keep everything slow.

Deirdre's relaxing;
Then rigid became, -
For Deirdre there's now
    A great deal of the same . . .

Deirdre is resting,
Her arms now enfold
A warm little angel
    So sweet to behold.

Joan S Henry

ALWAYS THERE

I'm merely a thought away,
It's not the closing of a life but the opening of another day.
I'm all around you on another vibration,
Here in this beautiful world of God's creation.
When you need me you only have to call,
I shall be there, lest you fall.
You sense my presence all around,
My love for you will never go to ground.
The tears, the pain, will eventually ease,
Until one day the world will begin to please . . . you again.

But time in this world is but a small measure,
And time is a gift we all should treasure.
Slowly go forward, feel no guilt but enjoy life again,
For sorrow is heavy, and too much of a strain.
The loss of my physical presence is so great to bear,
But know if you need me, in spirit - I will always be there.

Stephanie Elizabeth White

TAKE A BREAK

The sun-drenched beach
Sea blue embracing azure sky
Warm rays from the golden peach
Penetrating, as on the sand I lie.

The lush palms sway
Their leaves dancing on the breeze
Beautiful is surely my day
As a toucan calls from the trees.

Tropical is the feel
As horizon is kissed by the dusk
In the waves there plays a seal
As the flowers emit an aroma of musk.

The view is so heavenly
For what more could one ask
This really is the place to be
As my tequila I sip from a glass.

Back to reality I slowly rise
I reach once more for my brew
I wish to return so I close my eyes
It's amazing what a cup of tea can do!

Lisa Wakeham

GOLDEN GATES AHEAD

I gazed through the window while we waited outside. I heard a car turn up, was it him or just another guest? Eventually, it came, made from golden wood with handles at the sides. People crying, sobbing aloud. I could see my family crying silently as we all looked. The flowers on top were beautiful and we knew he would like them.

As we all walked in still and quiet, we heard the footsteps of the priest in front of us, with her head down and walking slowly. His daughters, son and wife sat at the front. All his grandchildren sat in the dark wooden seats behind, with the guests sitting way back, some had to stand but they didn't mind.

Hymns were sung and speeches were read. As the curtain went round, we all stared and sobbed as we saw him one last time before he went. His fellow friends crying at the back and the priest praying to the Lord as we walked out of the crematorium. We went to his wake and remembered all the good times he had and the ones we had with him.

My grandad.

Lucy Witherick (10)

CUCKOO CLOCK

Oh! You beautiful winged bird,
 To ask of you, to sing to me,
It would be most absurd,
 When all around, is naked tree!
 For winter is now.

The clock, must tick, must tock,
 Many times more . . .
Before, my ear I cock
 To hear the sound which I adore,
 When spring is here.

The dead leaves, of a season ago,
 Where my feet now tread . . .
Have turned to peat new flowers to grow . . .
 To give their glorious spread.
 Yes! spring is almost here.

Beckoned by the call, 'Cuckoo, cuckoo'.
 Flowers, laid to rest. Now reappear . . .
Daffodils, primroses, bluebells, shoot through . . .
 Their beauty, once more, for all to share.
 Yes! indeed, spring is here!

Peter W P Turner

TIDE OF TARMAC

Our country is being smothered by a tide of tarmac,
In years to come we'll say we want our farms back.
Once our countryside's gone, it's gone forever,
The nature of this land our grandchildren will know never.
They will look at all things man-made and austere.
But to me it has always been very clear,
That Beeching's drastic policy was so wrong,
We're missing those railway lines now they're gone.
The people he affected were not given a voice,
And now have to run cars, they have no other choice.
But if people were allowed to have their say,
They'd admit they don't want Britain to become all motorway.

A Cooper

UNFAIR DOG YEARS

My best friend's death relayed over phone,
Stroke took last breath, mind frayed all alone.
I dread going home, now his basket removed,
The joy we had, the tears he soothed.
We'd run in a cold winter, down the hills together slide.
Now his collar hangs on a coat hook, his lead limp by its side.
Every time I left the house, his forehead softly kissed.
Now there's no one waiting at the gate, my brother sadly missed.
I hope that God will walk him through the clouds each day,
He can wag his tail to lift me and clear the sky of grey.

John Clarke

DANCE TO A PLANETARY RHYTHM

The planets as they wend their endless way,
Match, in their style, your every thought and deed.
Though you may think you orchestrate your day,
It's you who follow where the planets lead.

At time of birth the cosmos marked you in
And registered each floating sphere its place,
Identifying you when you begin
To join the mortal coil and human race.

From then your mind and body interplay
With your environment and those within,
Unaware you're acting out each day
According to the great Creator's whim.

Because you're who you are and how you think
You will behave in just the way you must,
Ruled by the patterns of your cosmic link,
Energised by waves of solar 'dust'.

So, if quantum physics is not your game
Nor resonance and inverse square your line,
Like those of us who know not what to blame,
Say, 'Ah well! That's life!' And you're right every time.

John Daniels

THE FRIGHT

I see it in the corner,
I see it staring back.
Its legs are thick and hairy,
Its body's fat and black.

My head gets hot and sweaty,
My feet go deadly cold,
It's crawling close towards me -
So now I must be bold.

I have to calmly walk downstairs,
So I can tell my dad:
'Come quick, come quick, there's a bug in my room,
It's hairy, black and bad.'

So I rush downstairs,
Two or three at a time,
I grab my father's arm.
I rush upstairs,
Three or four at a time,
And fly into my room.

My dad gets the stool and reaches up,
I really am quite scared,
But then I hear a little 'squish',
Look up and nothing's there!

A Lawes (13)

I STAND AT YOUR BED

I stand at your bed
Hoping you'll wake up
And forgive the bad things
That I said
You're so ill
I didn't want this to happen
For you to run in front of that bus
I don't want it to be
The end of us
The reason why we were rowing
I thought you had a lover
Someone new
I thought I saw you kissing him
But now I know
It wasn't true
It was just your double
That caused all the trouble
I stand at your bed
Hoping you'll wake up
And forgive the bad things
That I said

Barbara Towes

I'VE TURNED INTO DAD

It was inevitable and it's sad,
But I've now lived long enough
To turn into my old dad.

I'm starting to have trouble
Climbing up the stairs,
And hate sitting too long in dining chairs.

There's a creak and twinge
In every bone,
And I really enjoy having a good moan.

I just barge past the 'youngsters' in
The supermarket queue,
And the things they say, turns the air blue.

And I hardly dare mention,
The fuss I make when at the Post Office
Collecting my pension.

But the bus pass comes in handy,
Especially when I go into town
And meet my friends for a 'shandy'.

While there I sit with them on one
Of the many benches,
I might be getting on, but I still
Cast an eye over the lovely wenches.

Bardon

WAITING

Beneath a lowering summer sky
Where barley blown the poppies hide
And surging hedgerows trump the cries
Of goldfinch guards who nest nearby.
Yet silence clasps this narrow way,
Banked in nettled hawthorn sprays,
And elder boughs beset with grass
And rusted wire-set concrete posts.

The scudding clouds concede a patch
    of clearest azure, swallow thatched;
Whose darting, weaves with tartan skill,
    the summer airs with whistled hues.
And dappled fields lift danken hearts
    and barley fringes dance their parts.

And yet their sounds another cry
That permeates this summer sky.
With hurried wisps of tumbled steam
Threading the weft of swallows' schemes,
Tumbling the edge-wise pastured walls -
Scatt'ring the rooks and grazing thralls.
And lowing, yet a distant thing,
Betrays an eager hurried gait
Climbing the hidden valley edge.

Till, bursting round the hawthorn screen,
    with flurried beat and billowing steam,
She thrashes 'neath the bridgèd lane and,
    restless, halts where farm hands came
These hundred rusted years or more - their gateway to a broader place.

And now, with wheezing pungent stride,
She tugs away her carriaged pride.
And silence settles this narrow way
Banked in nettled hawthorn sprays
And elder boughs and ruffled grass.
And signal set for none to pass.

John Rose

THE WAY TO A WOMAN'S HEART

To find the way to a woman's heart
Do I have to use my imagination?
I could buy her two dozen roses
For a special occasion.
I could give her expensive chocolates,
Buy her a diamond ring,
Or is the way to a woman's heart
In a love song that I sing?
To find the way to a woman's heart
Do I need a degree,
Because a woman's heart is sacred
And full of mystery?
I could give her perfume,
Buy her expensive lingerie,
Or is the way to a woman's heart
By saying you love them every day?

Robin J Grigsby

STROLLING . . .

Astride hedgerow stile, I pause a while
breathe deeply of woodland hue.
Pale sunshine, beguiles a smile
heart merges with nature renewed.

Primrose, beneath winter daunted trees
suddenly glimpsed, your sweet face.
Emerging through fallen leaves
in gentle act of faith.

Now with careful tread I stroll
towards a secret place, friends know.
Beside a stream, where in winter dreams
leisurely, summer kingcups grow . . .

Joanne Manning

THE WONDER OF NATURE

As bluebells carpet the shaded wood
The sun peeps through its thick green hood
Shafts of light where toadstools stand
Providing a platform for insects to land
Or a haven to hide under when it rains
As broken raindrops run down the lane
The scent and the colour are a beauty to behold
Walking through the bluebells standing so bold

Butterflies hover, seeming to have fun
Primroses on the bank the colour of the sun
Clusters of yellow bring delight to the eye
As the occasional rodent scurries by
Beetles under leaves with hard shiny case
Stay under cover when birds give chase
From branch to branch grey squirrels leap
And hedgehogs stir from winter's sleep

Children hold buttercups under their chin
It reflects bright yellow on their skin
Daisy chains are threaded sitting in a field
And for dandelion fairies there is no shield
They are blown through the air doing a dance
Wherever they land they take their chance
In brilliant sunshine or a misty haze
These wonders of nature never cease to amaze

Celia Law

THE DATE

Standing on the corner
waiting for my date
I am getting angry
for she is very late.

Do I really like her
I ask myself again?
Standing in this cold wet night
is really quite a pain.

I'll give her five more minutes
then I'll go and have a pint.
No girl mucks me about
although shc's a delight.

Suddenly she's at my side
she's such a pretty sight.
She's giving me that special look
I think tonight's the night.

John J Allan

PILGRIMS WAY

From Surrey's hills to Kentish downs,
    The pathway crosses hill and dale,
By rivers, woodlands, meadows green,
    It follows close that ancient trail.

This path they call the Pilgrims Way,
    Was once a Celtic route for trade,
From Winchester to Canterbury,
    They walked or rode by forest glade.

The Pilgrims came as years went by,
    To homage pay at Becket's tomb,
Knight and miller, friar and cook,
    In Chaucer's Tales each one found room.

King Henry made this journey too,
    On bread and water fed was he,
In sackcloth, ashes, penance made,
    Prayed for the Martyr on his knee.

Past Hog's Back, Newlands and Box Hill,
    By Chevening Park and Dunton Green,
Kit's Coty, Medway, Bluebell Hill,
    The wand'ring pathway tracks serene.

So on to Boxley, Detling Hill,
    Charing and Chilham we pass by,
Now sight the great cathedral clear,
    And know our journey's end is nigh.

Part bridle, pathway, track or lane,
    This age-old route we still can walk,
Avoiding crowded road and rail,
    Across those tranquil downs of chalk.

Geoffrey Elgar

SEAVIEW WALK

butterflies of many colours
red and yellow blue and brown
catch my eye with sheer delight
just away from Herne Bay town

along the seaview path meander
chat to folk who flutter by
strangers yet they have a light
beamed at being friendly, why?

here the sea meets with the land
one is mobile one is still
jolly waves dance on the sand
giving land folk such a thrill

lifted hearts all in a flutter
frames embraced by constant breeze
not unlike the coloured butterflies
who live their lives with ease

sea and rocks and sounds all foaming
white and grey and green and blue
pebbles sand and shingle groaning
shifting sifting as they do

so our nature's like big mother's
constant hues and shades of change
reflect a beauty like no others
invisibly, of a spiritual range

Bob Bedwell

THIS HAPPY BREED

(And you know who said that - Shakespeare's John O'Gaunt in Richard II. This poem inspired from Bill Bryson's book - 'Notes from a Small Island' page 98)

We may not realise this fact
Until it's pointed out
But just you watch and listen now
For sure there is no doubt.
It proves, when Britons have a chat
We must be happy folk,
For it's not long before we will
Be laughing at a joke.
We love our satire, quips and wit
To prove we have indeed
That sense of humour in us bred,
We are 'This happy breed'.

Valerie Small

EVER MINDFUL

The early morning dew, settled on the grass,
Crocuses and daffodils tell of spring at last,
The early morning chorus as the birds begin to sing,
We are so very lucky, we can hear and see these things,
The different greens of the countryside,
The beautiful blooming flowers,
The various shapes of the trees, mesmerise me for hours,
Hedgerows and the ploughed up fields,
Regimental and so straight,
Buttercups, daisies and dandelions,
Around the farmer's gate,
Horses gathered by the clump of trees,
Sunshine filtering through the leaves,
In the distance I can see a stile,
All makes me ever mindful
That I can see for miles,
Some folk, do not have the facility,
Of being able to see, these wonderful
Sights upon our planet, that are here for you and me,
Cows chewing the cud, they seem content,
Sheep and lambs with heads bent,
Chewing short grass that doesn't torment,
The steady throb of the tractor engine,
The farmer's out early today,
As the months go by, it won't be long,
Before he gathers in the hay.
The countryside is a changing scene,
Four seasons come and go,
I wonder what crop is growing there,
I'm afraid I really don't know.

John H Israel

WHEN WINTER MEETS SPRING

Glistening frost on barren trees
Sparkling droplets fall with ease
The willows hang like fairy gowns
With precious gems scattered round

Pretty droplets sparkling bright
Change to blue in warm sunlight
Beneath the willows cold and bare
Are tiny snowdrops growing there

Purest white their tiny heads
Like bridal gowns in which to wed
Silver ribbons left in the sky
As aircraft fly away on by

Lots of birdsong here and there
For now's the time for mating pairs
Two pigeons on the tallest branch
Bill and coo like a ballet dance

My garden's just a hundred foot square
But oh dear God, the wonder's there
Green shoots burst forth from frozen ground
Two robins feed on nuts they found

So many sparrows feast on fare
On table top and ground so bare
A squirrel runs from a hidden place
Hurry now or cats will chase

A heron stops for fish to eat
Shush away, for my fish to keep
Now a breeze is blowing
The frost but almost gone

It's powder blue on high Lord
I wish all the world could hear sweet birdsong

Susan Goldsmith

THE DANCE OF TIME

I can hear it moving, I feel it everywhere.
It saturates the sunlight, and adds aura to the air.
Something very precious, often misunderstood,
It hurries through the streets and alleys
Of every neighbourhood.

I feel the tempo in the way it moves
It is a rhythm I must abide.
With a lilt in my step and the wind in my hair
I dance the Dance of Time.

I hear the harmony in the clouds, the music sounding through the stars.
This is a power so easily free, it bursts from captivity,
Breaks all its bars.
As I look into the sky, so bright I am blind,
With a prayer in my heart and a smile on my lips
I dance the Dance of Time.

The flames in the fire flicker to the beat
The wild ponies follow it with their pounding feet.
On the high windswept hill the flowers all die,
But with a laugh in my soul and fire in my eyes
I dance the Dance of Time.

It is not an enemy but a friend, the aria follows you to the end.
The evening still echoes with memories of its song,
In the forest birds have chased it all day long.
The land retires and the night is all mine,
So with a glory in my spirit and wings on my feet
I dance the Dance of Time.

Ruth Wake

CALL ME JOHN - CALL ME WHEN YOU NEED ME!

I may be severely handicapped - but you'll see no misery,
The life that is forthcoming - will be entirely up to me,
To take up all the cudgels - to face whatever comes,
To make good use of fingers - so that I will not be 'all thumbs',
There will not be any whining - in my uttered sounds,
Of course there could be swearing - if trouble out there abounds,
I am not scared of fighting - for what is concerning me,
I will be staunch and forthright - in coming days you'll see,
I will be to the friendly - a most considerate one,
I will try always to be honourable - to myself and everyone,
I will be someone to depend on - no stupid kind of fool,
To the elderly I'll be open-minded - to the young I will be 'cool'.
Sometimes things might seem brutal - when others fail to care,
Whatever help is needed - you will always find me there,
There are many who consider - that we are useless to the core,
But once I have enlightened them - they will not think that anymore,
I may be frail and elderly - but if they think I'll wilt they will be wrong,
When I am opposing adversity - that's when I am most strong,
I am sure that folk will listen - most surely in the end,
When they realise that this old bugger - to them could be a *friend!*

John L Wright

BONNIE SCOTLAND

You speak of bonnie, bright Scotland,
of its lochs, its mountains and braes,
of the bright purple heather that abounds everywhere,
and the beauty there is to be seen.

The mists on the tops of the mountains
how it parts, and the beauty you see,
it gives, almost a glimpse of heaven
to the Scotsman, and also to me.

How I'd love to wake in the morning,
with the mountains and crags all around,
to feel such peace and tranquillity
with no-one else around.

To be alone with God on the mountain
where no phone or doorbell rings,
just, my Saviour and I
where mountain meets sky,
and I'd sit quietly, listening to Him.

I Davitt

BLACKBIRD

Little bird brave and bold
I will tend you in the cold
Sweet your song before you sleep
Till the dawn he does peep

Busy, busy all day long
But still you have the time for song
Back and forth to your nest
Juiciest grubs are the best

You're always there at my feet
Whilst in the earth I dig deep
When your work is well done
And you rest while others fun

Will next spring brave and bold
When snow and ice are long since old
Sing for me before you sleep
My heart will rest before dawn peeps

For in your notes there is gold
The riches wealth to untold

Susan E Roffey

NOISE

The song of a bird, the rattle of a train,
The dripping you hear when it starts to rain,
The crunching of leaves as you walk through the park,
The hoot of an owl when it starts to get dark,
The bang of rockets as they shoot through the sky,
The whimper of a pup as it starts to cry,
The creak of a door when someone walks through,
But how I hate noise when it's made by you!

Lucy Cross (12)

COMPASSION! (FIELDS OF EMOTION . . . MID-LIFE CRISIS)

In the anger of life's moment
when you make *another* cry
you feel the earth open
and wish that you could die.

In the eyes of your mistress
you see her last breath
as insanity takes you over
and you bring about her death.

In the view from your window
pollution clouds the frame
you spend all your lonely days
concocting a new and twisted game.

(In the midst of the night
when strangers pass you by
your only true ally
will be close to where you lie.)

In the fields of intense emotion
where the blood drains away
you stare into the vacant mess
where heroes often lay.

In the end you will admit
that your age was to blame
when you hang yourself in desperation
and she hangs her head in shame.

Bill Talbott

SEASONS THROUGH WINDOWS

A row of houses just near my way;
lots of windows, curtains bright and gay.
Children always in and out
lots of laughter, lots of shout.

After Christmas and New Year spree,
the weather is mellowing and the trees
are slowly awakening and sprouting,
at the windows children are waiting.

Waiting for running in the fresh air,
gathering spring flowers here and there.
After light rain, it is rainbow time,
through the windows the bright arched line.

Open windows, children's voices,
happy shrills, lots of noises.
It is summer, garrulous as the lark
children coming out, going to the park.

Summer gone, autumn approaching,
children at the windows are watching
the golden brown falling leaves
dancing madly in the chilling breeze.

Behind many a windowpane
little faces watching pelting rain;
Eager fingers at many heights,
tracing drops going left to right.

Closed windows, fires aglow,
children watching the falling snow.
Dreaming and making a plan
soon, to build a big snowman.

Licia Johnston

NATURE'S MONARCHS

Majestic trees, wherein their green and friendly bowers,
I spent so many, happy childhood hours,
firmly held twixt branch and trunk,
daydreaming, I was in a galleon's bunk,
or, standing up there so tall,
'twas my crow's nest and I saw all,
bound for adventure upon the high seas,
as the tree swayed gently in the breeze.

Under these monarchs, then a woman so young,
and love was new, my heart was worn,
where all was quiet and nothing would stir,
what wonderful balmy days they were,
our first love, what ecstatic wonder,
that nothing on earth could tear asunder,
we pledged forever, our love would be,
and half a century on, it still is, we.

Now our children and the next generation,
gaze at these giants with fascination,
then climbing as high as they will dare,
what a wonderful world can be found up there,
this wonderful gift from mother earth,
seems to share with us, the fun and mirth.

So, when I shuffle off this mortal coil,
and lie at rest in the encompassing soil,
beneath a majestic tree I'll lie,
its branches reaching for the sky,
but, even the tree under which I lay,
will some day wither and fade away,
until this time comes, I'll lie at peace,
blending through the tree, to its every leaf.

Audrey Packman

MOMENTS IN TIME

Today I sat in the garden,
you'd say, nothing wrong with that,
except that it was snowing, and
a magical moment at that.
Why do snowflakes have to melt?
They are peaceful moments in time,
a few more caught up in a spider's web,
lasted longer so were mine.
Their shape was symmetrical, six points
on every one, and yet they all were
different, like people just moments in time.
Find peace just like a snowflake, make
time to sit and be, balance your life,
less bustle with no hassle, and you'll
feel better just wait and see.

Twinkle

THIS FAITH OF MINE

What can exist?
Beyond this Earth of ours,
As the beauty
In a garden of flowers.
What to believe?
About human nature,
Since goodness sows
The seed of our culture.
How can we know?
The real purpose of life;
Some mock the truth,
We are the slaves of strife.
Never despair is a proverb to ease us;
Faith, hope and love are values of Jesus.
No one can shake this faith of mine;
Steps of being rise from design.
No one can prove there is no God,
Avoid the path that fools have trod.
Jesus taught; you must not be so blind,
Urging if you seek you will surely find,
The way, the truth, the Holy light.
Jesus insists you do that which is right.
So when you have discovered the truth divine,
You will also understand This Faith of Mine.

Maurice Webb

SORROW

Sorrow can be deep,
Devastating, desolating
And hurting.
Mindful of misery
Cannot see clear
Harping on hurtful words,

Mindful of hurt,
Hurt so great,
It feels heart is broken,
Broken into pieces
Never to be mending.

Until one dawn
Slight flicker of hope
Emerges from somewhere
Again to be squashed,

But from somewhere
Springs eternal hope,
Hope for better things
To come.

Riitta Pontela

MY DREAM

I went to sleep on a silent night,
In my bed snuggled up tight,
Closed my eyes and in a dream,
A rainbow shining a bright beam,
In Dreamland all my thoughts are true,
Don't you wish you were here too?
Flowers that have petals so bright,
The sky so blue, the sun so light,
Suddenly a flash of gold,
Then it quickly turned so cold,
I was back in my bed,
Snuggled up tight,
The stars were twinkling on a silent night.

Nicola Moulding

BLIND LOVE

Seven o'clock of the evening, I rap on the door,
The blindest of dates, I must take as a chore,
With butterflies twisting my innards asunder,
An apparition to appear, to regret as a blunder.

The seventeenth December, the year seventy-nine,
I await the door opening, view the evening mine,
Spy graceful a shadow, moving silently within,
The time of reckoning is about to begin.

May God be my witness, my heart is in my mind,
A vision of pure beauty, dark eyes smiling kind,
I stutter introductions, feeling awkward indeed,
My brother was right, she's just the lady I need.

Having travelled the world, and seen many a sight,
Loved many a damsel, though not with such might,
But something has happened, then, there, from the start,
For I've not lost just a voice, but also a heart.

Clifford M Loveland

THE MORNING CHORUS

Colours split into rays of sunlight,
Dreams are thrown off the edge of clouds,
Shadows echoing as they fall around my mind
Bouncing off rocks, dancing across patchwork fields.
Windows glinting,
Sunlight sends a spectrum pattern across the fields.
Musty corn is spread on a floor,
In the barn where a cockerel pecks distastefully,
Flowers open to greet the morning,
Feeling the warmth from the sun.
Melting like an up-turned butter dish
The day draws on,
Cows graze in a nearby field,
Horses shade under the big oak tree,
Its protective leaves fall onto the pond,
Breaking and shattering the still flat waters,
Changing them to a mass of swirling ripples,
Small birds paddle at its edge,
A solitary badger sniffs the air,
The day has begun,
Turning his back to the new day,
He returns to his sett on the hill.
Tall grasses start to sway in the breeze,
The sun slowly rises, golden light penetrates the sky, up, up,
Towering over the trees,
The morning chorus has arrived.

F R Divall

THE FIRST DAY OF SPRING

The fertile earth shakes off its frosty claw,
The nerves and tendons in its depths do thaw,
The oak and elm feel murmurings of new growth,
And nature rids herself of winter sloth.

The crocus seeks the sun with open face,
The spider weaves again her web of lace,
Beneath the rustic bridge the goldfish rise.
Forsythia strikes golden on the eyes.

The catkins shake their golden dust around,
Beneath the lilac, snowdrops now abound,
The whole earth from its slumber breaks,
And my soul from its winter gloom awakes.

Susan Widdicombe

THE ART OF LIVING

Through every simple brushstroke
On the canvas of our life,
The threads of possibility are etched.
Youth's palette-mix enhances
Our ability to thrive,
With optimistic hues of hope outstretched.

Yet, as layer succeeds layer,
To some permanence we cleave,
E'en images once certain seem far-fetched.
Shades and colours of our choices
With the unknown interweave,
And our portrait is irrevocably sketched.

Sue Morley

LANCING BEACH

Lightest of breeze
Sea in the air
Sounds of children
Playing down there.
Green on the shingle
Cabbage White
Occasional bird
In lazy flight.
Blue of the sky
Blue of the sea
White, wispy clouds
Soft, buzzing bee.
Shimmering distantly
Worthing pier
Sometimes hazy
Sometimes clear.
Moored on horizon
Fishing boats
Whilst nearer inshore
Swimmers float.
Out to the east
Brighton's sprawl
High in the air
A seagull's call.
Perfect now
The weather's fine
Lancing beach
In summertime.

Jeremy J Croucher

REQUIEM FOR A FAITHFUL MONGREL

He came to us as a puppy
Bob, we chose for his name
All he asked was our friendship
Our companion in sunshine and rain

He knew all the fields around us
He knew all the hills and dales
We traversed them together
On calm days and in gales

There was great trust between us
His steadfastness did not fail
He acknowledged a word of kindness
With a friendly wag of his tail

All creatures on this planet
Age as time passes by
And to our friend of eleven summers
It was time to say goodbye

Our Bob is not forgotten
He's in our hearts today
Still in his home here with us
And in the fields across the way

It was our privilege to know him
A dog who gave much joy
A man's best friend without a doubt
The mongrel we called 'Good Boy'

Fred Scott

TIME PASSING

How burns the fire? . . .
So hot, the flames dazzle,
And fierce warmth pervades the room.
The flames are gone,
Those dancing flames of youth,
Young love and joyous hope,
When everything told of tomorrow,
Of what was to be, so brave, so bold, so brash,
Joyous and so golden.
The confidence of youth rides on a charger,
White and spirited! Banners flying high!
Into the thrall of life!
But . . .oh but! how long before the veils of doubt, . . .
Of hurt, of punctured dreams,
Begin to fall, bruises come with quickening pace,
Hard blows seek to destroy that joyful mind, that happy soul,
For 'Time there is no stop'.
Spring to autumn turns, winter winds are cold and chill,
Too soon, it seems, bones ache, eyes dim,
No more the joys of yesterday.
The wise, fasten their coats and bow to the cruel wind,
For in the winter white a snowdrop blooms,
A leaf of green appears, and up above,
A patch of blue.
In the home the embers of the fire glow and give warmth,
And memories add consolation as the lesson of time passing
                                        helps to heal.

O Robinson

THE BATTLEGROUND

They tell us, when we're young, that all that glitters is not gold
But still we chase the rainbow's end for that pot of hidden treasure,
Don't stand there dreaming, get on with it, work hard is what we
were told
You'll be well off when you retire, and enjoy life at your leisure.

Democracy, capitalism, in whose name, great things are done
But who did pay the real price, since the day the allies won?
Was it the losers, whose occupation meant repair, renewal and invest?
Was it the victors, who paid the debt for clearing up the mess?
The proof is in the pudding, but with their economic success,
Who were the real winners, would you like to have guess?
Who arrogantly dictates to us, in the Euro Community,
Who from the east employs us, to make their cars so very cheaply,
Who profits from us, to help pay, for their higher standards of living,
Who remembers the price paid, those left who feel so deeply
Of the heroes who lost their lives, with courage and with giving?

Isn't it a funny old world, you often say, as you get little older
You've certainly learned that in real life all that glitters is not golden.

But there is still one overall, very non-political winner
That grand old lady Mother Nature, who always makes provision
For us to grow the things we need to cook and eat for dinner.

The golden sunset in the west, the golden sands for pleasure
The golden rod and daffodils, the songs of birds to treasure,
She works so hard to please us, from our youth, till we are old,
We should protect her, from the litter, so that she is always gold
We should always be there for her, and to pay her compliments
By going to war on those who try to destroy her Environment
So there it is that battleground so who will win again?
Will the winners be the losers? Or it does all seem, quite insane.

Molly Erkmen

TANK MAN

Hello Mister in your 4 by 4 waiting at the lights
Bet you haven't seen me standing here, up there at such heights
I wonder what you think about, as you drive around in that tank
Can you really afford it, or is it really owned by the bank?
Is that why you got it? So we think it is something you can afford
The lord of the manor touch, a few rungs up from my rusty old Ford
The engine does sound impressive, I don't know, but I expect it's a V8
Now I hate to say this chap, but you don't look very happy as you wait
Your expression doesn't say 'Look at me I've made it!'
You are so forlorn and don't look like you are enjoying it a bit
I expect you are a very nice man and visit your mother every Sunday
Or maybe you give all your spare time and money away
I know, as I walk over this crossing I'll give you a smile
Will it rile you I wonder if someone like me dare look at you a while
I'll try and radiate a bit of happiness and let's see how you react
But I warn you mate I'll judge you, it's my only guide as to how you act
Let's see how you respond from a happy gesture from a pedestrian
Will I pass your approval and if so what I wonder will Sir test me on
So here we go and I'll watch your face and let's see what appears on it
Wow, well that to me says more than what you got under that bonnet

James Barry

THE PANE

She stares impassively out of her window,
Her reflection is all she can see contrasting to the dreary weather.
It has changed over the years but the inner child still remains.
Lingering, waiting for a chance to emerge from the hidden,
                  almost forgotten depths of her mind.
That window has seen the sorrows, happiness but most of all memories,
Memories of a child's hands on the clean pane.
She no longer stares at her reflection but looks out of the window,
A small smile works its way across her lips,
The old record playing in the background reminds her of the old times,
A thousand lights on the polished floor, the large skirts and the dancing,
Those were the days,
Every cloud has a silver lining.
So many memories.
Now as she looks across the suburbs and the vast network of roads
        which, in her time, were rolling hills covered in trees,
What will the future hold?
She blows on the window and then puts her hands on the misty
                    pane and remembers,
Memories clouded like the window yet still the light shines through.

Samantha Olive

EACH TIME I CRY

Each time I cry a tear for you
The memories flood right back
Of sunlit walks along the shore
Or dashing for a mac,
When sudden shower blots out the view
And grey crowds out the blue.

Each time I cry a tear for you
A little stronger I become.
Now I must do for you what's due
In solitude must be.
Don't let your memory leave me, dear:
My heart can't break anew.

Each time I cry a tear for you
God sends an angel down
To wipe my eyes of passion's dew
And take away my frown.
The path I tread is strewn with rocks,
But I shall take the knocks.

Next time I cry a tear for you
I'll think of your sweet smile
And hair of chestnut hue;
Your gentleness and patience all the while;
The way you died with happiness;
Our one last kiss of closeness.

George Alexander

A GHOST IN THE WIND

Through broken faces and a wintry blow.
A spirit surfaces,
Whose evil lurks from above,
A fatal blow, an innocent act
Torn in between, the black and white.
Demons from distant pasts,
Inner torment, painful memories.
As time goes by, broken promises,
Angered rage, revenge on the present be.
Back to the past. Face through a twisted journey,
Give and take through mortal minds,
Lack of freedom a selfless act,
Imprisoned inside.
Lonely, as drifting through shreds of time.
Redirected by a mysterious force.
Ongoing as life yet untold.
Fatal images,
The picture of the untold word.
Whose time is it now?
Turning back, led astray,
Only once a mistake . . . ?
Time has come to think,
Now before, a past must be,
Not a punishment but an apology.
Now it has gone . . .
It's always there in the back.
Resting, imprinted,
A part of the whole.

Chris Fenton

PANDA IN THE STONE

Undulating journey,
halted by the square house
centred in nesting doves.

Returning trees line the solid
narrow road opening to the sea
and shore where, stooping, we
find the panda in the stone
underfoot.
Accidental image, alert,
elderly, earnest, unhurried,
with eyes of a dancer.

Underfoot;
fallen from eroding,
sky-blocking, chalky cliffs.
Flint of flints
millions tide shifted,
feet shifted,
containing stories.
Mysteries of history,
creation
turned to hard, cold stone
warmed
in the palm of a hand.

Jane Bingeman

BOOK POWER

What is it about books
They fascinate me,
To see them in the bookcase
With different coloured spines,
Some with ornate and fancy designs.

There are cookery books
With a wide range of ideas,
There is even a book of various beers,
I just sit and browse
Great ideas within me house.

Books that make you read on and on,
What will happen next?
How will it end?
How much further will the story extend?
I still keep reading, it's gone past lunch,
I must finish this book till it comes to the crunch.

Gardening books, oh how exciting,
How to make your garden inviting.
Flowers and shrubs, they give pleasure,
For the birds plants with berries,
Flowers for the bees,
Plants to attract butterflies, life is a breeze.

I love books, I could sit there for ages
Just flicking my way through all the pages,
Sitting in my favourite place
Having an adventure without taking a pace,
Books, they add character to a home.

Margaret Kinshott

TIGER, TIGER, SHINING SO BRIGHT

Tiger, Tiger, shining so bright,
   Stalking your prey in the shadows of night.
Beautiful coat of orange and stripe,
   Threatened species. The gun goes snipe.

You roam the jungle so proud and so great,
   To be killed for coat and bones is a cruel fate.
With governments which just don't care,
   The poor tiger can only despair.

Tiger, Tiger, what a cruel fate,
   For you and your cubs, and your handsome mate.
You have such a beautiful face,
   And you move with such stealth and grace.

In the jungle you fight tooth and claw,
   Yet the lion is the king of the jungle law.
But with your magnificent power and size,
   The tiger must take the jungle prize.

Elizabeth De Meza

To Mum And Dad

Simple acts of love were these
They fill my earliest memories
The endless watching of my 'plays'
The annual Caister holidays
Picnics in the park and red bus rovers
Handmade dresses and Dad's pullovers
Putting me up on my first horse
Regretting it in due course
As hour after hour on a leading rein
I'd make my dad trot a fat pony up a leafy lane

Our home open to all my friends
During the summer that never ends
Giving me my purple bike
Walking Joey our dog on the Sunday hike

When I had been bad Mum threatened me with Dad
Dad the monster coming home
Sending me to my room alone
'I'll count to 10,' said a voice like thunder,
By the time he'd reached five I'd buckled under.

Now I'm older they're still the same
Whenever I needed them they came
Whenever I cry they dry my tears
Allow me to air my worries and fears
Encourage me to do my best
Help me out with every request
No matter how mad my scheme
Or how precarious my plans may seem

They never question me too much
Never want to be out of touch
With whatever's going on, be it right or be it wrong
The door's always open
The kettle's always on
They're always there to rely upon.

Joyce Quinnell

NARCISSISM

Narcissism, a perverse prism,
Turns all colours white;
But the purity of a blank canvas
Gives poor comfort in the nihilistic night.

James Helling

DANBURY HEIGHTS - A PLACE TO PAUSE

It may be that you of the gentler past
Knew of our need, who come on dusty roads
Blind with reflected sunlight, driving fast,
Almost ignoring, weighted down with loads,
Into the magic of your sudden calm.
Perhaps you thought, a hundred springs ago,
When, undisturbed, the birds sang in your trees,
And trembling reeds stood near the waters low
And many bees hummed in the flowered leas
That we, despoilers of the fruitful earth,
Might snatch a moment from our crowded days
To find the peace of which you knew the worth
And muse awhile with undistracted gaze;
Then you made here, upon this rising ground,
Where the city ways bring hurrying travellers by,
A place to pause, where willow trees look down
In waters that smile back into the sky.
Here a small cottage welcomes us to rest
And offers comfort with the cup that cheers
And we discover that your thought was blessed
Who thought of us, across the vanished years.

Marion B Alford

SOLITAIRE

When I reveal the game I play is solitaire
Friends remark that to myself I'm not being fair,

To which I reply, nothing with it can compare,
It's the most thrilling of games, one which few would dare,

Believing the single state is impossible.
Too few strong enough to be that invincible

To withstand the pressures that are put upon them,
Or the claim from 'two's company' all pleasures stem.

But I play this game simply to avoid the strife
I prefer to do without in this short life.

My character would suffer much diminution
If I got hitched, fettered in this institution.

I'm happy, contented with my own company.
I get around, spared duties and anxiety.

The domestic scenes I see make me want to scream,
The bickering and backchat like some squalid dream.

It's all so uncivilised, what I most dislike,
Such behaviour exposing the dark side of life.

Too often have I watched the rows between my friends,
The stress, the grief, the bitterness that always rends

A family apart, stricken before it all ends,
The hassle that follows trying to make amends.

The wear and tear so awful it's hard to repair,
All too often leads to sad and lasting despair.

Far too much can go wrong when two take marriage vows,
It's a strict contract that no much leeway allows.

If one rides roughshod over the other's feelings,
It can lead to violent fights, or legal dealings.

You take a final step putting your faith and trust
In another who could well cause you to go bust,
Sequestrate your income, sue you for your last crust.

Laura Edwards

REVELATION

She stared at him,
her mirror,
watching her
observing him.

She didn't like parts of him,
her mirror,
aspects of herself she abhorred
he acted out.

She acknowledged his darker side,
her mirror,
stepped forwards into the light,
he followed.

She watched him wrangle with change,
her mirror,
butting his head stubbornly against the future,
confused.

Impatiently he desires what she has achieved,
his mirror,
so reaches out to snatch his illusion,
empty-handed.

Looking to her for answers,
his mirror,
to find gaping emptiness -
his own reflection.

Jannine Howe

UNTITLED

The sea is the devil of all mankind,
It can break your soul and lose your mind.
The waves roll over - again and again,
They've caused so much trouble and so much pain.
So many went out there - the good and the brave,
They fought the almighty and went to their grave
Fighting the enemy with all their might
Under the stars that shone so bright.
They went in, the thousands waving the Union Jack,
But so many were killed and only a few came back.
Those poor sailors, what they did was for mankind,
Now they want us to forget them and leave them behind.
Think of the families of the deceased
And leave them alone to rest in peace.
Those brave men, they fought those glorious fights
On those wicked seas on the darkest of nights.
They deserve to be remembered for what they did for us all,
The strong and the mighty and the small.

Carol McCann

MASSACRE

Half a million sheep lie still
their pyres already lit
to join the carcasses of cows
and lambs that once were fit.
A shepherd with his guiding crook
stands silent on the plain
staring at the massacre
and sharing others' pain.
In separate herds the deer
creep by with velvet, wary eye,
treading grassy paths to reach
a mountain steep on high.
Little fawns on bracken sleep
waiting for the dawn
and stars that twinkled
now do weep forlorn.
Into the killing night
where peace on earth
was wrenched unmercifully
by massive blight.

Ann Safe

IMAGES OF CHRIST

I recall when I was a child long ago
In my imagination I would be
Watching Christ perform His miracles
Beside the sea of Galilee.

I would be one amongst many
Enthralled by the things He did
Just a small child at the edge of a crowd
It was all in the mind of a kid.

When I grew into adolescence
I no longer had time for such childish notion
I had real people around me
To give me real love and devotion.

Life seemed to hold such promise
I was on the crest of a wave
Till a drunken driver one night
Sent me to the edge of my grave.

Confined to spend months in a wheelchair
I seemed to float on a sea of despair
Back through the years to my childhood
To find Christ still standing there.

Again I stood a child amongst many
But this time it wasn't the same
Christ held out His hand towards me
Softly He called me by name.

A nurse asked me why I was smiling
How could I explain convincingly
Although I had forgotten Christ
He had not forgotten me?

I am now fully recovered, no more depression no pain
But this I know for certain I will never forget Christ again.

Gwen Liddy

QUINTESSENCE, OR FATHER'S FIVE FACES

Dad - The Miner

Rivulets of sweat turning dust into mud, the coalface *no*
parlour of beauty,
Eyes red-rimmed and swollen through fug and fatigue, and an
eight-hour shift of dank duty.
Like a flock of Welsh 'blackbirds' released from the cage they
flew down the ramp - homeward bound,
No baths or hair-dryer to clean off the mire, but just glad to be up -
safe and sound.

Then lamps handed in with a joke and a grin, and Dad at the head of
the throng
As proud as can be, flanked by Tom, Elfed, me, he smiled as we
burst into song.
Steel tips keeping time on the cobbles, 'Cwm Rhondda' the
favourite choice,
E'en the larks in the sky gave way by and by to the lilt in Dad's
clear tenor voice.

Dad - The Preacher

Immaculate on Sunday in shiny black suit, with glistening starched
collar - shirt rubbing-board white,
Carbolically clean from black hair to white feet, he strode to
Caersalem - the devil to fight.
A god of a man was my father, the pulpit his heavenly choice,
With women seduced by his ardour and all hypnotised by his voice.

He lambasted sinners for drinking, and women for flirtatious ways,
He threatened them hell and damnation, eyes afire with devotion
and praise.
They loved it, and came back each Sunday, I don't know how
many he 'saved'!
A god of a man was my father, by the way that he worshipped, behaved.

Dad - The Musician

Like a train coming out of a tunnel (steam wonders that once used to
be)
Were sopranos that Dad taught each Sunday as they struggled to
reach that top 'C'.
My dad was a wonderful teacher, he knew all there was about scales.
His choir won all the Eisteddfods, his pupils were famous in Wales.
A Doctor of Music with Honours, his scores oft composed
underground,
His hymns are still sung in the valleys, although he's no longer around.

Dad - The Father

He never laid hands on his children, his eyes - disapproving - enough,
He was quiet - but stern - not grim-visaged, but we never tried
calling his bluff!
A brilliant musician and scholar, he was offered a job in the States:
He'd have gone like a shot, but Mother would not, if he'd gone he'd
be one of the 'greats'.

There was always good food on the table, plain fare - but enough
to go round,
For he'd take any job to earn a few bob, with workers stood
off underground.
He 'got on his bike' in the General Strike in search of pastures new,
To seek out better prospects - for his children as they grew.

'Twas Dad the father humping bricks and wheeling barrows of sand
That built our brighter future in England's 'Promised Land'.

Dad - In The Hereafter

Now Father's passed on to a land filled with song, I pray God's
a judicious employer
And knows that He's got the best of the lot to look after the
heavenly choir.
I could tell a million stories of my father in his prime,
His sacrifices and his love - if I only had the time.

John Elias

WHY?

Why can't they see things from my point of view?
Why do they say the things they do?
Why can't I change it?
Why do they treat me this way?
I don't know what to do or say?
Why is life this way?
A week seems like forever and a day.

Nicole Woollard

CANTERBURY RIVER

Shimmering glittering, murmuring, rippling,
Under the bridges where children play pooh sticks,
Running, laughing, shouting and giggling,
Deep in the shadow of great stone towers,
So massive, ancient, lofty, unchanging,
The gates of the city still standing through time,
And the river runs on through the shops and the houses,
Onward, eternally on to the sea.

Shimmering, glittering, murmuring, rippling,
Inside the river the weeds are like eels,
Sliding, tangling, flowing and streaming,
Marking the path of the water where fishes,
Shining and sparkling, yet shadowy, secretly
Play and then die in their shining wet palaces
Deep in the unchanging water that changing runs
Onward, eternally on to the sea.

Helen Marsh Jeffries

A DAY OFF

Oh work again, I just can't face it
Really don't want to get out of bed
It's raining, I think I'll phone in sick
And say I've got a cold in the head
Ha ha, they swallowed that one OK
Another half hour and I'll get up
And decide what to do with my day
It's so cosy, but I must get up
I should go downtown and pay some bills
And get in some much needed shopping
Get washed and dressed, see how I feel
Oh come on now and don't keep stopping
Whoops, it's ten o'clock, I must get up
If only to make a cup of tea
Fumble for the sugar, milk and the cup
I've made it to the chair, oh lazy me
So this is what they put on TV
During the day while I'm out at work
Get up now, stop being so lazy
A good English fry-up, that will work
That was great, I'll get dressed in a mo
Maybe tidy up the house a bit
Another cup of tea, then I'll go
Still raining, maybe I'll forget it
Who says I have to do anything
After all, work is just one long slog
Sometimes it's great just to do nothing
Boy, I must have needed a day off.

S P Chesterman

THE GENTLE TOUCH

Lord I feel your tender touch,
When I am low, it helps so much
You take my will and make it Thine
And then I lose my decline.
I see the stars - no dark clouds anymore,
But instead, a lovely 'silver shore',
Due to your wonderful healing hand,
It's then I walk the 'golden sand'.

Margaret Enwright

ANCHOR BOOKS
SUBMISSIONS INVITED
SOMETHING FOR EVERYONE

ANCHOR BOOKS GEN - Any subject, light-hearted clean fun, nothing unprintable please.

THE OPPOSITE SEX - Have your say on the opposite gender. Do they drive you mad or can we co-exist in harmony?

THE NATURAL WORLD - Are we destroying the world around us? What should we do to preserve the beauty and the future of our planet - you decide!

All poems no longer than 30 lines.
Always welcome! No fee!
Plus cash prizes to be won!

Mark your envelope (eg *The Natural World)*
And send to:
Anchor Books
Remus House, Coltsfoot Drive
Peterborough, PE2 9JX

OVER £10,000 IN POETRY PRIZES
TO BE WON!

Send an SAE for details on our New Year 2001 competition!